Booker T. Washington: The Life and Legacy of the Famous Civil Rights Activist

By Charles River Editors

About Charles River Editors

CHARLES RIVER
E D I T O R S

Charles River Editors provides superior editing and original writing services across the digital publishing industry, with the expertise to create digital content for publishers across a vast range of subject matter. In addition to providing original digital content for third party publishers, we also republish civilization's greatest literary works, bringing them to new generations of readers via ebooks.

Sign up here to receive updates about free books as we publish them, and visit Our Kindle Author Page to browse today's free promotions and our most recently published Kindle titles.

Introduction

Booker T. Washington

"Men may make laws to hinder and fetter the ballot, but men cannot make laws that will bind or retard the growth of manhood. We went into slavery a piece of property; we came out American citizens. We went into slavery pagans; we came out Christians. We went into slavery without a language; we came out speaking the proud Anglo-Saxon tongue. We went into slavery with slave chains clanking about our wrists; we came out with the American ballot in our hands. Progress, progress is the law of nature; under God it shall be our eternal guiding star." – Booker T. Washington

From 1890-1915, the most influential black man in America was Booker T. Washington, who less than 35 years earlier had been born into slavery. The young boy worked laboriously until emancipation before going on to seek an education, and by the time he was 40, he was consolidating a network of supporters that came to be known as the "Tuskegee Machine," helping coordinate action with the support of black businesses, religious communities, and others. Using his position of power, Washington spoke out against Jim Crow laws and Southern disfranchisement of blacks.

Despite being so recognized, and perhaps in part because of it, by the early 20th century, Washington's tactics were questioned by other black leaders, notably W.E.B. Du Bois, who wanted to protest more vehemently in an effort to secure civil rights. Washington, 12 years Du Bois' senior, entered the field of education and founded the famous Tuskegee Institute based on his vision of what a population emerging from generations of slavery required in order to successfully integrate into modern life. His position was simply one of incremental entry by the provision of industrial education and political accommodation. He urged blacks to accept discrimination in the short term and concentrate on elevating themselves, thereby proving themselves through hard work and material prosperity. Du Bois would have none of that, believing it amounted to an approval of the Jim Crow regime of the South and a passive acceptance of racism. In opposition, he and other black leaders organized the Niagara Movement, citing opposition to Washington's moral leadership of the movement and marking their determination to fight for full civil equality for black Americans. The movement did not gain much traction, but it was in direct line of ascension to the much more influential National Association for the Advancement of Colored People (NAACP).

Washington believed confrontation would only hurt the cause, and that cooperation and softer tones would wear down racism over time. Ultimately, both men wrote voluminously in support of their stances and thoughts. Washington wrote 14 books, including his renowned autobiography, *Up From Slavery*, which was published in 1901, and he continues to be recognized for helping to improve the relationships between blacks and whites, as well as helping blacks get further access to education and civil rights.

Booker T. Washington: The Life and Legacy of the Famous Civil Rights Activist chronicles the life and work that made him one of America's most influential men. Along with pictures of important people, places, and events, you will learn about Booker T. Washington like never before.

Booker T. Washington's Childhood

"You can't hold a man down without staying down with him." – Booker T. Washington

The history of slavery in early America remains widely referenced in the modern age by familiar phrases such as the nation's "original sin," or its "fatal flaw." Whether discussed in the framework of government structure, economics, or social politics, the founders' inability to resolve the matter has thrown the American psyche into an unceasing conflict, threatening not only the Union's tranquility, but in specific eras its very existence. By the outbreak of the Civil War, a bloody legacy of the 18th century's failure, racial conditions had only worsened, and the Declaration of Independence, with its overt assertion of universal human equality, remained a mere wish list of Enlightenment ideals in terms of practical American life, particularly in the Southern states. The Constitution had offered no provision by which an individual could be classified as a lesser or partial citizen, but the ugly truth to the contrary was undeniable. Stephen A. Douglas argued against Lincoln for a balance of free and slave states in an effort to maintain the national status quo as the country gathered wealth and power. Such a policy, he hoped, would remain the norm as new states were established. Lincoln, on the other hand, sensed the inescapability of a continental reckoning with the practice, and called for its immediate elimination. The ensuing war confirmed that the United States was no more prepared to reach a resolution than it had been at its creation.

The Civil War's aftermath, despite the Union's victory, brought its own brand of horror for black people in the South. Following proposals for repatriation to the African continent, a move actually braved by a few, the pre-war slave class was here to stay in numbers too large to ignore. The only alternative for these residents was to seek full citizenship and social equality, a long uphill climb for a segment of the population originally brought from overseas to serve as beasts of burden. The period commonly known as Reconstruction produced a state of civil abuse as violent and dangerous for black residents as war had been for soldiers. Jim Crow laws served as an effective substitute for slavery. The defeated South remained staunch in its efforts to preserve the antebellum social hierarchy, moving the war to its own streets and fields. Instances of lynching became rampant while opportunities for improved living conditions were walled off from virtually every pursuit in which an adult African-American might forge a living wage. With high courts upholding the Jim Crow scheme, "separate but equal" became the South's accepted structure, insisting on the former while violently preventing the latter. Such conditions endured into the early 20th century, expressed at times through traditional hostility, but just as frequently through collectively informed silence.

The men who emerged as spiritual and political leaders for black people born in the Civil War era initiated an ongoing debate on the pursuit of equality. Black men addressing white audiences on political and social matters were to remain an extreme rarity, so for many years the conversations and conflicts were honed within the venues of black culture. Tenets and strategies within the equality movement produced a racial think tank, a hybrid of spiritual, intellectual, militant, and vocation-oriented forces, and two starkly contrasting paths emerged in the quest for racial equality.

In the first years, open rebellion took a back seat to an elevation of vocational expertise in order to recast black Americans in a new and improved light before the eyes of white society. The anticipated rewards saw the former slave class as newly educated, intelligent, reliable, and less threatening. Within such an undisturbed social equation, the black family was to freely participate in the nation's economic fortunes, gaining access to professional advancements once deemed an exclusively white domain. In time, black workers were intended to merge with white society in the marketplace, and find release from Jim Crow restrictions, including unfettered voting rights.

Conversely, the second, a more confrontational approach, demanded instant equality with an already sensitive white population dreading a mass uprising on their doorsteps. The insistence of immediate inclusion in education, politics, and corporate involvement came from charismatic young firebrands, many of them preachers and professors from outside the South. The church, among other institutions of the early 20th century, was a prime vehicle for social mobilization in at least the emotional sense. In tandem with spiritual unity, the development of black intellectualism was intended to challenge white predominance in pursuit of executive levels of employment and to encourage the pride of outright ownership.

The living conditions and racial status of Booker T. Washington at his birth offered scarce promise of later accomplishments as "one of the most influential intellectuals"[1] of the late 19th century. Birth records were notoriously scarce or inaccurate even for white citizens in many of the country's rural areas, so it's no surprise that for a boy born only a few years before the Civil War as a slave, the odds were a good deal steeper against confirming a date. Washington himself professed ignorance of his own childhood, but April 5, 1856 is an accepted consensus. His birthplace is generally designated as Hale's Ford of Franklin County, Virginia on a farm of 207 acres near Smith Lake. His owners under the law at that time were James T. and Elizabeth Burroughs. The prophetic first name of Booker remains a mystery, but the middle initial of his owner signifies the Taliaferro family, prominent in the highest Virginia circles.

Washington was a mulatto slave, and the general assumption holds that his father was a white man from a plantation somewhere in the region, but since slaves were being bought and sold at will with no regard for the preservation of cohesive families, it is doubtful that Washington knew his entire family. Indeed, as an adult, he professed total ignorance of his ancestry or anyone outside his immediate family. As the major economic system of the nation revolved around factories, the South remained largely agrarian, and in this environment, the geographical range of a farm slave's working life in the South could be considerably larger than the confines of an

---

[1] Eric Foner, John A. Garraty, *Booker T. Washington*, History.com – www.history.com/topics/black-history/booker-t-washington

immovable factory occupying a city block.

Washington's mother was known only as "Jane" until 1860, when she married Washington Ferguson, a slave from a nearby plantation. Soon after Ferguson's marriage with Jane, Washington's stepfather escaped to West Virginia. Outside of an encounter at Christmas, the family did not see him until the Civil War's end. Jane Ferguson gave birth to three children, but there may have been others who were sold in the region. Washington's older brother John was also a mulatto, with the lighter complexion and light gray eyes of his younger brother. His white father remained unidentified as well.

As the plantation's cook, Jane's cabin of approximately 14 x 16 feet was used as the estate's general kitchen. In his childhood, Washington never saw a wooden floor and never slept in a functional bed, instead relying on nothing more than "bundles of rags,"[2] regardless of the season. His daily dress included a flax shirt which he recalled as having been as painful as chestnut burrs. Washington later wrote, "I cannot recall a single instance during my childhood or early boyhood when our entire family sat down to the table together, and God's blessing was asked, and the family ate a meal in a civilized manner. On the plantation in Virginia, and even later, meals were gotten to the children very much as dumb animals get theirs. It was a piece of bread here and a scrap of meat there. It was a cup of milk at one time and some potatoes at another."

The overriding frustration of Washington's youth was being barred from attending school. Reading for black slaves was discouraged and eventually made illegal in the South, so the closest he could come to a schoolhouse was to carry books for Laura Burroughs, daughter of the family and a teacher. However, the oncoming war and secret meetings with an 18-year old Ohioan named William Davis living with the local Baptist pastor allowed Washington to develop some reading skills.

South Carolina was the first state to secede from the Union, followed by others in rapid fashion. 5 of the Burroughs' sons soon left home to fight for the Confederacy, which left Mrs. Burroughs with no sons at home, a complement of 10 slaves, and a difficult regimen with blockades preventing access to traditional foods. Even the traditional Southern coffee was concocted from a recipe of parched corn. The deteriorating situation did not impact the slave population as much as it did the whites who were accustomed to luxury and shaken by its loss.

The entire force of workers at the plantation broke into celebration as the arrival of emancipation was declared on a momentous day in 1863. Washington recalled his mother's ecstatic state as a stranger arrived to read a speech, presumably Lincoln's official proclamation. He also remembered the brevity of the elation as the coming responsibilities of being free set in within minutes. He noted, "As the great day drew nearer, there was more singing in the slave quarters than usual. It was bolder, had more ring, and lasted later into the night. Most of the

---

[2] National Park Service, *Booker T. Washington* – www.nps.gov/a-birthplace-that-experienced-slavery-the-war-and-emancipation.htm

verses of the plantation songs had some reference to freedom... Some man who seemed to be a stranger (a United States officer, I presume) made a little speech and then read a rather long paper—the Emancipation Proclamation, I think. After the reading we were told that we were all free, and could go when and where we pleased. My mother, who was standing by my side, leaned over and kissed her children, while tears of joy ran down her cheeks. She explained to us what it all meant, that this was the day for which she had been so long praying, but fearing that she would never live to see."

Getting an Education

"I have learned that success is to be measured not so much by the position that one has reached in life as by the obstacles which he has overcome while trying to succeed. Looked at from this standpoint, I almost reached the conclusion that often the Negro boy's birth and connection with an unpopular race is an advantage, so far as real life is concerned. With few exceptions, the Negro youth must work harder and must perform his tasks even better than a white youth in order to secure recognition. But out of the hard and unusual struggle through which he is compelled to pass, he gets a strength, a confidence, that one misses whose pathway is comparatively smooth by reason of birth and race." – Booker T. Washington

For Washington, emancipation represented not so much a sudden social liberty as an opportunity from which he might obtain the education formerly denied him. He was 9 when he was emancipated, and his family moved to Malden, West Virginia shortly after, where he was reunited with his stepfather. Among the first gifts he received from his mother following emancipation was a spelling book, and he had enough free time to teach himself the alphabet fluently.

The family's state of poverty still ruled out an elementary school education. Ferguson saw no need of formal education for a former slave child, and he dismissed his stepson's zeal to attend when a local black school opened nearby. Instead, Washington was set to work packing salt into barrels and spent full shifts in the coal mine. He turned the regimen of the factory into an asset, using the numbers printed on the salt containers to learn basic arithmetic. Eventually able to circumvent Ferguson's edict, he arranged to attend the new school at night.

In time, the salt furnace job he so despised gave way to a gentler form of employment when he was taken on as a house servant for a white family. Washington claimed in retrospect that this was his first opportunity to learn the virtues of "frugality, cleanliness, and personal morality,"[3] according to the dictates of the ruling class. Other than during his time with the Ruffner family, his childhood and early youth lived in the war years offered no moral or intellectual training.

Louis Ruffner was the owner of the mine in which Washington had worked, and through his

---

[3] History.com

wife Viola, he sensed the chance to better his position. After carrying books for the Ruffner daughter, teachers and students noticed him lingering around the schoolhouse, and Viola Ruffner allowed him to attend school for one hour per day. The hour was his first experience with formal education. Socially shy and lacking a pedigree, the idea of being the only student with one name was a source of shame. He added the name Washington himself, and he continued using it for the rest of his life.

As Booker Taliaferro Washington, the teen's confidence was bolstered, and his zeal for a full-time advanced education grew more intense. His employers were surprised to hear that at the age of 16, Washington intended to leave them in an attempt to secure a spot at the Hampton Normal and Agricultural Institute several hundred miles away on the shores of the Chesapeake. To attend a school of such magnitude was a far stretch for a boy still dealing with incomplete literacy, but he was resolute. Accomplishing most of the distance on foot between successful intervals of hitchhiking, he arrived at the doors of the Institute looking utterly disheveled, and in possession of only 50 cents in his pocket. Given that he hardly seemed to be the ideal model of a Hampton student at first glance, Washington was first confronted by an unconvinced principal, Miss Mackie, but he persisted while student after student gained admittance before him. Taking note of his patience and restraint, and eventually sensing the potential in him, Mackie asked him to sweep one of the classrooms. Washington instantly complied. Apparently approving of his work, Miss Mackie allowed him to enter school, paying his way as the campus janitor. In later years, he fondly referred to Mackie's request as his "college examination."[4]

Money earned as a janitor was sufficient for paying room and board, and for the next three years, he was up at dawn to stoke the fires for every classroom. According to the general code of the institution, Washington correctly perceived that his conduct from the outset was the internal model for the way a former slave should act. The Institute taught the virtues of a respectable outward appearance, which required not being prone to vanity, as well as a constant demonstration of respect and civility. The pursuit of money as a single-minded goal was discouraged, as overt wealth was considered the gateway to personal corruption and unhelpful for improving the community.

During his three years at Hampton, Washington strove to perfect his oratory skills by participating in the debate society, learning to advance the equality agenda without emotional intensity or threat. Using his own story at Hampton in later writings, Washington installed himself as both the ethical narrator of the message, and the protagonist in the behavioral model. The adoption of a respectable and respectful demeanor at all times doubtlessly informed his later approach to the search for full citizenship.

Daily life at the Institute was, in material terms, everything Washington's childhood was not,

[4] Patricia Daniels, *Booker T. Washington, Black Educator and Founder of Tuskegee Institute*, Thoughtco.com, April 7, 2017 update – www.thoughtco.com/booker-t-washington-1799859

and he described it as a "constant revelation."[5] He was served regular meals daily, complete with a tablecloth, an utterly alien concept for his social status. Sleeping on an actual bed every night, he marveled at the idea of sheets, covers, and using a personal toothbrush. If anything, to Washington, the manner in which he was invited into the Institute was in itself a blueprint for encounters with white society, high-minded thinking, and expertise in essential skills.

Among the many individuals Washington admired at Hampton, General Samuel Chapman Armstrong, its founder, was the one he held in the highest esteem. Armstrong founded the school four years prior to Washington's arrival with the mission of providing "moral training and a practical industrial education"[6] to each of its students. A graduate of Williams College in Massachusetts, Armstrong rose through the Union Army to command an African-American unit in the war. Intensely anti-slavery, he worked with the Freedman's Bureau, adding Native Americans to the student enrollment list in subsequent years. Armstrong stood out as Washington's model of how best to provide a practical education for blacks in America, and he would later employ the same tactics himself in the establishment of future institutions. Hampton was run much like a military academy, and it stood as one of the most disciplined learning environments of its time. In his autobiography, Washington described Armstrong as "a great man, the noblest rarest human being it has ever been my privilege to meet."[7]

[5] Jim Powell, *Up From Slavery: A Biography of Booker T. Washington* – www.libertarianism.org/publications/essays/slavery-biography-booker-t-washington

[6] Black Past.org., *Hampton University (1868 - -)* – www.blackpast.org/aah/hampton-university

[7] John Simkin, *Booker T. Washington*, Spartacus Educational – www.spartacus-educational.com/USAbooker.html

Armstrong

At his graduation in 1875, Booker T. Washington was a featured speaker, and in addition to the audience of faculty and students, a *New York Times* reporter was present. He praised the speech as being extraordinary for someone so young.

Many such graduates might have succumbed to the pull of the city and previously untested career paths, but Washington returned to Malden in an entirely different position. He spent the year of 1876 as a teacher at Tinkersville School, of which he was an alumnus only a few years prior. Taking on a demanding schedule, he taught classes for hundreds of students, including for children during the day school and adults at night. Washington had by this time apparently realized the full dimension of his life's dream, but barely three years after arriving in Malden, he abruptly resigned from the school and entered the Wayland Seminary, a Baptist theological school. His precise aim in making such a transformation was unclear, but the change of career did not suit him, and he left Wayland only six months later. The episode was an inexplicably sore subject on some level - he scarcely ever spoke of it again, and others were cautious about asking.

The answer may lie in what historians term the Compromise of 1877, although others dubbed it "The Corrupt Bargain"[8] or the "Great Betrayal."[9] Through this agreement, Reconstruction ended and the South was returned to "home rule,"[10] opening the way for Jim Crow laws that would dominate across the region for the next 75 years. The presidential election of 1876 left both major parties in a dilemma, as Democratic candidate Samuel J. Tilden won the popular vote and led in the Electoral College, but did not have enough electoral votes to secure the win over Republican Rutherford B. Hayes. The constituents of both parties were fatigued by the corruption of the Grant administration, and eventually, a commission consisting of Senators and Supreme Court Justices was convened to settle the matter. Republicans offered to remove all federal troops from the South if Hayes was named president, and Democrats promised to uphold and respect black rights. As the party of former slave and plantation owners, Democrats failed to uphold their end of the bargain, bringing a reign of racial terror to the South. Such a shock to the nation's social system must have jolted Washington to his core, and he replaced theological priorities for work on serious temporal issues of equality.

A string of opportunities refining Washington for that purpose began with Armstrong's invitation to join the faculty of Hampton. A teaching job at his alma mater was not anticipated, but his invitation to speak at the 1879 spring commencement produced such a fine speech that a position was offered on that day. Again, Washington included night classes in his regimen, and they were among the most popular on campus, tripling the night enrollment within a term.

---

[8] American Historama, *Compromise of 1877* – www.american-historama.org/1866-1881-reconstruction-era/compromise-of-1877.htm
[9] American Historama
[10] American Historama

Tuskegee

A picture of Washington as a young man

"I think I have learned that the best way to lift one's self up is to help someone else." – Booker T. Washington

Washington's time at Hampton might well have been the crowning professional moment for a former slave, but he was caught up in the movement of black education by a recommendation to oversee a new school dedicated to a vocational curriculum in the South. Armstrong again served as inspiration, as Washington was sent to Tuskegee, Alabama to organize and oversee a bold new program set in one of the most antagonistic enclaves in the country.

As a skilled conversationalist, informative and unthreatening, it was Washington's job to diffuse fears among the general public that former slaves were rising too far in station. Past that, he was required to extol the virtues of agricultural and industrial skills as a benefit to white society. Once accomplished, he was mandated to erect a physical facility where one did not yet exist.

In a sense, Washington had to explain his own presence before anything else. The commissioners who sought out General Armstrong by letter, certain "gentlemen of Alabama,"[11] had requested a white teacher. No alternative had crossed their minds, so Armstrong took it upon himself to convince them that Washington was truly the only one he could comfortably recommend, and they ceded the point. Among the first commissioners to meet Armstrong was Lewis Adams, a skilled artisan in several crafts from his former slave days. As an African-American, he likely possessed little doubt that a black headmaster could fill the position admirably. However, he may have assumed that a white principal was at the time a given.

Adams

Adams' participation came about through two local political candidates, William Foster and Arthur Brooks, both of whom sought his help with the black vote. In return, they promised support for the school. Adams delivered on his promised assistance, and the politicians kept their word. His fellow commissioner, George Campbell, was white and a former slave owner. In assisting in the establishment of the school, helping to find land and bringing Washington aboard, he displayed an unusual example of timely social enlightenment. What was eventually

[11] Richard Wormser, *Booker T. Washington, the Rise and Fall of Jim Crow*, Thirteen: Media with Impact – www.thirteen.org/wnet/jimcrow/stories_people_booker.html/

brought from nothing but a handful of ramshackle buildings on a deserted farm to a prestigious institute and later a respected university, stands as "a monument to his life's work."[12]

The physical work required to raise a school was daunting. Washington was recommended and hired for an institution that did not exist. The legislature approved a modest $2,000 per year for faculty salaries, but nothing else. Washington responded by first incorporating the construction of a campus into the curriculum. The first student assignment was to clear 540 acres of wooded land in order to grow crops. With a group consisting of former slaves, children, or grandchildren of slaves, most took to the work, however reluctantly, and everyone involved in construction of the school worked from dawn to 9:30 at night. A few were teachers in their own right from small villages in the region, and felt that such labor was beneath them. Changing such perceptions was to become a cornerstone of Washington's aims, that there is nobility and dignity in work. Once a down payment of $200 was secured, the still small student body went to work. The main building, a farmhouse, had burned down years before. However, a few of the original structures were still upright, including two cabins, a horse stable, an outhouse, and one henhouse, which was later employed as a classroom. The first desks and blackboards were made on campus by the carpentry department. Many of the students were destitute, and they could not pay for either tuition or lodging. From this dilemma, Washington adopted the Hampton model of students entering into labor on behalf of the collective in exchange for room and board.

What eventually rose out of the field was nothing short of impressive. The first new building, the center point of the later campus, had three stories and contained a chapel, library, and living quarters. In the first year, Washington amassed 112 students and three teachers.

---

[12] D. Barry Croom, *Agricultural Education at the Tuskegee Normal and Industrial School*, North Carolina State University – www.files.eric.ed.gov/fulltext/EJ840076.pdf

Washington's house in Tuskegee

A picture of a history class at the school

The idea of training his students in necessary vocations for the region was not only a component of Washington's core beliefs, but an immediate necessity. The great bulk of the student body was illiterate, so it almost goes without saying that training a new student in Shakespeare, foreign languages, or higher mathematics was a leap too far. In Washington's model, all knowledge imparted, regardless of the subject, was required to be couched in agricultural and industrial terms and themes. By requiring English, mathematics, and history teachers to decrease their study load in favor of pursuits closer to rural life, he instituted a process called "dovetailing."[13] Any assignment not merged in some way with this aim of the curriculum could result in severe reprimands or termination for teachers. Through this link to regional realities, Washington intended to eliminate "learning for the sake of learning."[14]

Later critics of Washington's vocational approach wondered whether he had inadvertently created a glass ceiling for his students by restricting them to low-level employment far from the benefits of ownership or management. Such drawbacks were not Washington's intent, and Tuskegee's founding was based on the premise of training teachers to further disseminate vocational skills. Rather than fearing the rise of black authority in the South, many whites viewed the school as a tool by which to convince blacks to accept their inferior conditions and

---

[13] D. Barry Croom
[14] D. Barry Croom

status. Had he sought to instill a cosmopolitan sophistication in his students, the time-worn theme of blacks parading as whites might well have changed the equation. The successful intellectual model of Fisk University in Nashville, already well-established, did not fit Washington's model for social inclusion and equality. Rather than preparing a student body capable of competing in such an erudite atmosphere, Washington's more grounded purpose was to "transition a race of people out of slavery and into citizenship."[15] He was of the consistent belief that in the fight for black equality, "economic self-determination" should come first, before civil rights activism.[16]

As he moved farming, carpentry, masonry, and other life-related subjects into the center of the curriculum, intellectual critics assailed him as the "Great Accommodator," and accused him of ignoring the burdens of segregation and Jim Crow laws. To protect his institute from an easily threatened white populace, Washington never overtly criticized segregation, leading some to assume complicity on his part.

Despite rejecting the activist model for black advancement, he nevertheless diverted secret funds in opposition to Jim Crow. His care for tending the school's relationship with white society was directly related to fundraising, at which he excelled. Creating the impression that the school was a solution to white/black conflict rather than a black movement, he garnered donations from Southerners as well as prominent Northern philanthropists. Providing the bulk of funds, benefactors north of the Mason-Dixon Line included Pennsylvanian Anna T. Jeanes, one of 10 children from a dry goods and coal mine family. When the last sibling died and Jeanes inherited the family fortune, she immediately set up a million-dollar fund to "educate and hire"[17] black teachers and supervisors throughout the South, and to improve facilities. Washington was installed as one of two trustees, and he helped distribute funds for "Jeanes' teachers."[18]

Henry Huttleston Rogers, a Massachusetts industrialist and major figure in Standard Oil, joined Washington's cause in 1890. New Yorker John D. Rockefeller, founder of Standard Oil and a "devout Baptist,"[19] spent some of his $500 million philanthropy on Tuskegee. Rockefeller, Rogers, and Carnegie espoused the "Protestant work ethic" as a central tenet of black advancement in the South. At the same time, those from other faiths were more than competitive. Jewish business giant Julius Rosenwald of Sears Roebuck built 5,000 schools that came to be known as "Rosenwald schools"[20] throughout the South to benefit black youth. In addition, he funded the hiring of 14,000 teachers and the building of 4,000 libraries.

---

[15] D. Barry Croom

[16] History.com

[17] NNDB, *Anna T. Jeanes* – www.nndb.com/people/0761/000204461/

[18] NNDB, *Anna T. Jeanes*

[19] Encyclopaedia Britannica, *John D. Rockefeller* – www.britannica.com/biography/John-D-Rockefeller

[20] Sears Archives, *Julius Rosenwald* (1862-1932) – www.searsarchives.com/people/juliusrosenwald.htm

Rogers

Critics, while hailing Washington's best efforts, complained his success was all too dependent on white money. In some cases, such criticism may stem from a racial embarrassment that black people could not yet fully fund their own rise. To others, it meant the continued domination of white overseers capable of controlling an agenda or curriculum. However, no credible evidence exists that Washington ever let loose his iron grip on any matter pertaining to Tuskegee. Selective in choosing his battles and showing his political cards, Washington was "self-assured and influential"[21] when it came to emphasizing economic self-reliance before violence. He narrowed his vision to education and racial respectability, acting as the "foremost black educator, power broker, and institution-builder of his time."[22] As a network of support to Washington's regimen of "industrial and moral education,"[23] and for his public school teachers, he established a wide net of schools and black newspapers that came to be known by critics as the "Tuskegee Machine." Their purpose was to serve as a voice against Jim Crow.

---

[21] History.com

[22] History.com

[23] History.com

Despite the propensity of these sources to trumpet a rebellious tone instead of having Washington risk it himself, nothing involved with Tuskegee was done without his blessing. That he did not protest in the streets or at the pulpit as a more modern activist brought the charge that his wily dealings with racial enemies revived the notion that his was nothing more than a "doctrine of accommodation."[24] As such, those unable to look beneath the surface of his work only saw that he surrendered to social and political inequality, and advocates of a parallel and conflicting ideology came to characterize him as a coward. However, the camp calling for Americans of African descent to help themselves and to reject all other assistance was trapped in a problematic reality. While black people could summon the intelligence, the will, and even the organizational prerequisites for a social rebellion, they had from the beginning been shut out from access to money. The leap of faith to forego the massive financial assistance from whites would have required surrender to utter powerlessness. Tinkersville, Hampton, and Tuskegee would likely have never materialized.

1882 was cause for celebration on two fronts. Washington witnessed the completion of a large new building on campus, and in August he married Fanny Smith, a former pupil at the school in Malden. Smith had grown up in the town, and the two were likely acquainted at an early age. She is said to have been part Shawnee, and her Christian name was interchangeably spelled as Fanny or Fannie. Hailing from a rural environment with few opportunities, she nevertheless managed to attend day school with 80-90 fellow students, under the tutelage of Washington.

Like her teacher, Smith was accepted into Hampton against steep odds, and the two courted there. However, Fanny was forced to leave after falling behind in tuition payments. Returning to Malden, she taught classes to save for completing the curriculum at Hampton. During this period, in which she served as her mother's primary caregiver, she managed a daily three-mile walk coming and going. After two years, she sent the final payment of $48.00 to Hampton and resumed her studies there. After she graduated in 1882, Smith and Washington were married in Rice's Zion Baptist Church in the Tinkersville section of Malden. She was 24 years old, only two years Washington's junior. Relocating with her new husband to Tuskegee, the couple took on four faculty members as boarders, and Fanny acted as the institute's housekeeper, although her influence on the school was more extensive. She is credited with "broadening the curriculum for female students"[25] by establishing a home economics program. When the endowment increased, Washington hired her for other duties, and she is said to have been particularly effective in fundraising efforts such as dinners and benefits. In 1883, the couple's only child, Portia Marshall Washington, was born. However, in May of the same year, Fanny mysteriously died of unknown causes, making Washington a widower before the age of 30. She was interred at the Tuskegee University Campus Cemetery.

Tuskegee soon gained statewide recognition and became a source of pride for Alabamans

---

[24] History.com

[25] Newikis, *Fannie Smith Washington* – www.newikis.com/en/wiki/Fannie_Smith_Washington

within a short period. Part of the institution's instant success came from a public demonstration of the various disciplines under study. To teach farming, carpentry, blacksmithing, and building construction was one thing, but the students proved the overall merit of the approach by growing their own food and constructing their own buildings. Housekeeping, sewing, and mattress-making paralleled the men's studies, and the excellence of Tuskegee's brick-making raised its prestige in town and rural areas.

Every avenue was explored in touting the accomplishments of Tuskegee beyond the borders of Alabama. Washington went so far as to organize the Tuskegee Singers, eventually growing into a refined vocal ensemble that toured the North, including wealthy areas where choir members would never have been granted permission for residence. Such appearances represented startling transformations of perception for those whose first image of an African-American was an illiterate, disheveled slave.

In the spring of 1885, 80 students proudly graduated from Tuskegee, and soon after, Washington married again, this time to Olivia A. Davidson, a 31 year old Tuskegee teacher of four years. Once married, Olivia was appointed "lady principal"[26] of the institute. Davidson offered much assistance, as Fanny had, but her skills as an educator and administrator were unusually keen. In fact, some describe her as a "quiet co-founder"[27] of Tuskegee. Teaching by the age of 16 in Ohio and Mississippi, her years at Hampton coincided with Washington's, and they were both selected as speakers at the same commencement. Her scholarship to Hampton was personally underwritten by First Lady Lucy Webb Hayes. Washington and Davidson were married in August of 1886, and she joined the faculty of Tuskegee not only as a teacher, but as a "curriculum specialist."[28] Her teaching load included mathematics, astronomy, and botany. The couple had two children, and Portia became Olivia's stepdaughter. The two sons were named Booker, Jr., and Ernest. However, fate was again unkind to Washington. Olivia's health began to show signs of fragility after the birth of their second child, and she was sent to Boston for medical help. She died on May 9, 1889 of what was then called tuberculosis of the larynx. Washington had lost two wives in six years, before the age of 40.

---

[26] Patricia Daniels, *Booker T. Washington, Black Education and Founder of Tuskegee Institute*, thoughtco.com, April 7, 2017 update – www.thoughtco.com/booker-t-washington-1799859
[27] AAREG, *Olivia Davidson Washington, Quiet Co-Founder of Tuskegee*, November 11, 1854 – www.aaregistry.org/story-olivia-davidson-washington-quiet-cofounder-of-tuskegee/
[28] AAREG, Olivia Davison Washington

Olivia

The following year, Washington presented a speech at Fisk University in Nashville, one that was to exacerbate the latent criticism of his apparent accommodation to aristocratic white society. It further strained the relationship among leading figures of black congregations in the South, a group with which he had previously fared well. In the speech, Washington took on black ministers as a unified group, charging them with being "uneducated and morally unfit."[29] When confronted with an unexpected backlash, he refused to retract his statements. The incident was a step toward looming black divisions in the equality movement.

Four years after becoming a widower for the second time, Washington married once again. He met Margaret James Murray at the Senior Dinner of Fisk University. Like Olivia, Margaret was an educator and administrator, also a reformer and clubwoman. Born in Mississippi, either in the same year as Washington or as much as four years before, she was the daughter of a slave and unknown Irish father. Her exemplary work at Fisk won her a position at a Texas college, but she opted for Alabama and Tuskegee. As Olivia had, Margaret became the school's "lady principal"

---

[29] Patricia Daniels

responsible for the female students. Surprisingly, it was not Washington who brought Murray to Tuskegee, but Anna Thankful Ballantine of the staff. Cases of hiring staff members without the direct intervention of Washington were rare, but he had already begun courting the candidate.

Unlike Fanny and Olivia, Margaret was decidedly "reluctant"[30] to accept his proposal. She intensely disliked one of his brothers and was equally put off by the primary caretaker of Washington's children. If she proceeded with the marriage, she would become their stepmother. Washington's daughter Portia would have none of it, being "outright hostile"[31] toward anyone who attempted to replace her mother. Despite these barriers, Murray eventually accepted, and the two were married on October 10, 1892. As vitally important to Tuskegee as Washington's two former wives, Margaret extended the institution's vision by founding the Women's Industry Division while teaching domestic skills. When Washington's fame increased, so did his travel itinerary, and Margaret served as Acting Head of the School while he was away. They had no children together, but the couple adopted Margaret's orphaned niece several years later. Margaret went on to found the National Association of Colored Women, and she was president for four years before colliding with the same wave of activism that so often attacked her husband's work. Due to her sympathies with his gentler approach to the equality movement, history has often glossed over her accomplishments and central importance among influential black women.

---

[30] Jone Johnson Lewis, *Margaret Murray Washington, First Lady of Tuskegee*, Thoughtco.com – www.thoughtco.com/margret-murray-washington-3528124

[31] Jone Johnson Lewis

Margaret

Washington with his wife and sons

Leadership

Washington circa 1895

Washington's address at Fisk was controversial, but it would certainly not be the most controversial of his career. In 1895, he was invited to speak in Atlanta at the Cotton States Exhibition, during hwich he presented an unveiled rejection of black activism, a call for collaboration with white society, and a directive for African-Americans to bloom where they were until greater opportunities for advancement were created. At the time, many blacks were in a desperate search for a new figurehead, as the legendary Frederick Douglass had died only a few months before, and for those who favored the peaceful, collaborative path, Washington was the ideal candidate. The enduring phrase from his Atlanta address, called the Atlanta Compromise Speech by many, was a plea to "cast down your bucket where you are."[32] To protect black individuality, he suggested that blacks could be "separate as the finger, yet one as the hand in all things essential to mutual progress."[33] The most difficult part of collaboration to sell to black people was the nobility of manual labor, and the dignity of working the land. Declaring that "no race can prosper till it learns that there is as much dignity in tilling a field as in writing a poem," followers responded that they had done just that since being enslaved in the new country. Backbreaking work was not the goal of most black families, who were understandably desirous for the luxuries and relaxed life available to wealthier citizens.

---

[32] History.com
[33] History.com

In this way, the mission statement of Tuskegee did not necessarily translate uniformly to every audience. Nevertheless, Washington was, for a time, a giant among black leaders as activism continued to fight for its majority. To these men, Washington openly questioned why one should take up militant resistance to something that could not possibly be defeated, but which could be angered to the point of responding with horrific retribution. He described activism as an "artificial forcing"[34] of natural change. Rather, as whites and blacks increasingly worked together, familiarity would erode suspicion and discomfort. The white population would eventually give the black businessman a chance as he came off the farm a proven success. Only then would ownership and full upper-level participation be possible. However, until then, Washington was adamant that "the agitation of questions of social equality [is] the extremist folly."[35]

During this period, Washington often spoke three times per day, but while no black businessmen advanced and the "familiarity" was not readily apparent, support for him among other activists began to deteriorate. White support, on the other hand, was rabid, as the former slave class was to settle into its proper niche and be content with its lot. So content was the white response to a speech filled with lofty goals but no racial threat to the status quo that President McKinley paid a personal visit to Tuskegee soon after. For those seeking accommodation, Washington's words were taken as a "bonfire of salvation,"[36] rivaling the Emancipation Proclamation itself in some quarters. To critics, however, Washington perpetrated the fatal flaw of a collaborator, that of acting as a spokesman for two races. According to Louis Harlan's research on the era, such divided allegiance suggests that Washington "is certainly the most controversial Negro ever."[37] Harlan wrote a notable biography of Washington and two volumes pertaining to his materials, and he eventually won a Pulitzer Prize in the process.

The Atlanta speech caused much debate, and some violence. Those favoring collaboration clung to their shrinking majority, and some black Americans returned to the African continent. As for making history, Washington's speech in Atlanta was the first case of a black man addressing a large body of Southern whites. Even those who took the address as a call to "trust paternalism and accept the fact of white supremacy"[38] understood that Washington was not a weak, indecisive man. To the staff and students of Tuskegee, he was gratefully classified as a benevolent despot with his finger on every piece of the institute's minutia, a success story in the mold of Horatio Alger. To whites, Washington was the "model of humility and ingratiation,"[39]

---

[34] Richard Wormser

[35] Richard Wormser

[36] Donald Calista, Booker T. Washington: Another Look, *The Journal of Negro History*, Vol. 49 No. 4 (Act., 1964), University of Chicago Press Journals, pp. 240-255

[37] Sherman Jones, Review of Booker T. Washington: A Powerful and Multi-Faceted Politician by Louis Harlan and Raymond W Smock, *Change*, Vol. 14, No. 3 (April, 1982) pp56-58

[38] Robert A. Gibson, *Booker T. Washington and W.E.B. Du Bois: The Problem of Negro Leadership*, Yale New Haven Teachers Institute – www.teachersinstituteyale.edu/curriculum/unit/1978/2/78.02.02xhtml

[39] Robert A. Gibson

what many saw as a more well-groomed, polite form of old slavery. Philanthropists from North and South hailed Washington as the "chief exemplar and spokesman"[40] of his race, and the key to normalized relations. A master of "political adroitness,"[41] whites created their own impression that Tuskegee would keep the young black population "down on the farm."[42] Hard-driving Northern industrial giants walked away with images of a new, more sophisticated labor force, willing to follow through on their groundbreaking projects. The black people at home in Alabama and throughout the South envisioned a way by which they might escape share-cropping and follow petit-bourgeois aspirations similar to those of lower middle and middle class whites.

Washington continued to teach all groups drawing from his own life. Scholars could debate at will whether his success was created by slippery accommodation or through collaboration and good will with no ulterior motives. Regardless, even as an educator, Washington was not working in the abstract on exotic or unreachable subjects. His people would be required to work in the fields and town infrastructures first.

Tuskegee's prestige gained international recognition when famed scientist and inventor George Washington Carver joined the faculty. Like Washington, Carver was born a slave. To direct students toward careers in science may have been, in Washington's thinking, beyond the reach of those from slave origins, but in Carver, top-tier science met practical agriculture, the subject most dear to Tuskegee's mission. While members of the faculty were pooling their resources and living in single buildings together, Washington hired Carver through the allure of a "hefty salary,"[43] private rooms at the school, and relatively luxurious working facilities. The modern city-dweller might wonder at so much attention being given to the lowly peanut, but Carver's discovery of over 100 products "using one major crop"[44] was a major industrial boon to the South and to the country at large. Employing the same research for sweet potatoes, soybeans, and pecans, the Tuskegee labs produced a plethora of products in general use to this day. Uses for the peanut, outside the field of nutrition, have reached 300, including "milks, plastics, paints, dyes, cosmetics, medicinal soaps, ink, and wood stain."[45] From the potato came "molasses, postage stamp glue, flour, vinegar and synthetic rubber."[46]

---

[40] University of North Carolina, *Documenting the American South* – www.docsouth.unc.edufpn/washington/bio.html
[41] University of North Carolina
[42] University of North Carolina
[43] Biography, *George Washington Carver* – www.biography.com/people/george-washington-carver-9240299
[44] Biography, George Washington Carver
[45] Biography, George Washington Carver
[46] Biography, George Washington Carver

Carver

Carver's accomplishments proved a great boon to both Tuskegee and Washington. On June 24, 1896, the same year in which Carver was hired by Tuskegee, Harvard College conferred on Washington an honorary graduate degree. The honor was not lost on either Harvard or the press, announcing that for the first time, the prestigious institution "confers an honorary degree upon a colored man."[47] According to the *Journal of Education* in an 1896 statement, Washington's high degree of popularity affirmed that he was the "foremost living man of his race."[48] His premier accomplishment was cited as "the creation of an educational system adapted to Southern conditions, more than anyone else."[49] As was customary, Washington took the opportunity to speak on the "economic fallacy"[50] that underpins the idea of a subservient class. Like tying the hands of a valuable collective resource, economic barriers to work and ownership were in

---

[47] BTW Society, Booker T. Washington Society, *Honorary Master's Degree Conferred by Harvard College*, June 24, 1896 – www.btwsociety.org/library/honors/01.php

[48] Journal of Education, *Booker T. Washington*, Vol. XLIV, No. 13, 1896, Trustees of Boston University

[49] Journal of Education

[50] Journal of Education

Washington's words "a discouragement of thrift."[51]

In the same year, a landmark Supreme Court case all but enshrined Jim Crow in the South. Four years earlier, Homer Plessy, an African-American train passenger, refused to sit in an all-black car. Claiming that his civil rights were violated, the case reached the Supreme Court as *Plessy v. Ferguson*, testing the "separate but equal" theory at play in that era. The court ruled that the status quo was not racially based, but that it "implies merely a legal distinction"[52] between the races, and that the 13th and 14th Amendments were not violated. Only one jurist, Justice John Marshall Harlan, dissented.

The case opened the floodgates for the imposition of overtly racial Jim Crow laws in the South. African-American voting rights were all but obliterated through poll taxes, literacy tests, violence and intimidation. Black residents of the South were trapped in a cycle of debt, and learning to read again became a violation of the law.

Such a widespread regional edict struck at the heart of Washington's mission, and nothing in his response could have been construed as "accommodating." Putting his donor base at risk, he described states in the South with high concentrations of African-Americans as "a cancer gnawing at the heart of the Republic."[53] He maintained that the Republicans' former support of black equality, one of the very reasons the Civil War was fought, had dissipated, and that the Republicans had abandoned the mission for the sake of a false national unity achieved at the expense of black people in the South. Washington believed they were enabling a "white reign of terror"[54] to be unleashed.

In 1899, Washington took his first vacation since the founding of Tuskegee almost two decades earlier. In a three-month tour, he sought physical restoration, but he could not deny his interests in European solutions to American problems. Similarly, he could not avoid European discussions of the American situation. A simple vacation resulted in numerous speeches, and personal conversations with the likes of Mark Twain and Queen Victoria. He took great interest in the farming system of Holland, in which farmers in that country maintained efficient living standards on surprisingly small plots of acreage. However, even among liberal acquaintances, he downplayed his response to the tragedies produced by Jim Crow at home. Asked to comment on the murder of a black man from Georgia who was "strung up and burned alive,"[55] he declined to comment, offering only his belief that over time education would eliminate such atrocities.

Washington's response to Jim Crow was both predictable and seemingly rational. He believed

---

[51] Journal of Education

[52] History, *Plessy v. Ferguson* –www.history.com/topic/black-history/plessy-v-ferguson

[53] Jim Powell, *Up from Slavery: A Biography of Booker T. Washington* – www.libertarianism.org/publications/essays/lavery-biography-booker-t-washington

[54] Donald Calista

[55] Patricia Daniels

that underneath the most important pillars of society, including religion, an essential economic prosperity was required. To that end, he founded the National Negro Business League in 1900 as a direct counter to Jim Crow despite taking no actions of overt resistance, and allowing it to occupy itself only with commercial matters. With the assistance of Andrew Carnegie, the official launching was held in Boston, and membership was open to elite and middle class businessmen. This included doctors, lawyers, insurers, educators, and agriculturalists. In a magnified network of the sort with which he surrounded Tuskegee, Washington brought into play a long list of national black organizations, including the National Negro Press Association, the National Association of Funeral Directors, the National Negro Bar Association, the National Negro Insurance Association, the National Negro Retail Merchants Association, the National Association of Negro Real Estate Dealers, and the National Negro Finance Corporation.

Carnegie

A picture of Washington and Carnegie at Tuskegee

In the same year, Washington set about writing a set of memoirs, not merely to be employed as an archive, but as a functional catechism for black equality. He hired a writer to help him begin, and the end result was *The Story of My Life and Work*. Despite sales of 75,000 copies, a disappointed Washington referred to the work as a "rush job."[56] He subsequently hired Max Bennett Thrasher, author of *Tuskegee: Its Story and Work*, to make a second attempt, with Doubleday's Water Hines assisting. The introduction was penned by Washington himself.

By 1901, a vastly improved book, *Up from Slavery*, was in publication, and the memoirs exerted a significant impact on Tuskegee's major donors, some of whom did double duty with his Business League. As an emblem of a successful year, Washington sent a check to John D. Rockefeller as a refund for finishing one of his Tuskegee buildings under budget, and during the same period, he was able to make secret payments to New York lawyer Wilfred Smith to challenge the practice of barring black citizens from juries. Shortly after, Washington accepted an invitation to the White House to meet with President Theodore Roosevelt, who often sought Washington out for advice on racial conditions. Incensed by the presence of a black guest at the White House, a white backlash created a furor of protest that "stung"[57] Roosevelt to the point that he never again issued such an invitation. However, Washington continued as an advisor on political appointments for the subsequent administration of William Howard Taft. More accepted than ever by white elites, Washington received a second honorary degree in 1901 from Dartmouth University.

---

[56] Jim Powell
[57] Patricia Daniels

A picture of President Roosevelt and Washington at Tuskegee in 1905

When Alabama passed an alteration to the state constitution that disenfranchised potential black voters, Washington stuck to the business at hand and made no overt protest. Stepping up his work with Thomas Fortune, owner of the *New York Age*, he published a ceaseless supply of stories and editorials favorable to himself, the work of his school, and to the goal of equal prosperity. Fortune's publications were of such value that when the paper found itself in financial trouble, Washington became a secret member of its principal stockholders. He arranged for his autobiography to be reprinted in *The Outlook* magazine, appearing with an updated title. Support for his work continued, although critics argued that the ideology of the memoirs represented nothing more than the prevailing white American view.

Washington in 1903

Differences of Opinion

"My experience is that people who call themselves 'The Intellectuals' understand theories, but they do not understand things. I have long been convinced that, if these men could have gone into the South and taken up and become interested in some practical work which would have brought them in touch with people and things, the whole world would have looked very different to them. Bad as conditions might have seemed at first, when they saw that actual progress was being made, they would have taken a more hopeful view of the situation." – Booker T. Washington

By the early 20th century, what had initially started as a difference of opinion in the pursuit of black equality eventually became a fracture between those in favor of vocational self-help and militant activists. W.E.B. Du Bois, who had once accepted the Atlanta Compromise Speech with only mild protest, ignited a war against Washington's economic model as patience wore thin. In his own defense, Washington reminded his critics that they were laboring in an entirely different world that afforded them numerous intellectual luxuries not workable in the South. Similarly, Washington knew blacks in the South could not count on support from any governmental or financial body. The black congregation displayed no cohesive movement as citizens hunkered to withstand the Jim Crow wave. What Du Bois could express publicly in the North was grounds for lynching in the South.

Du Bois

Willian Edward Burghardt Du Bois was born in Great Barrington, Massachusetts, and he was Washington's junior by over a decade. A natural scholar, he was raised in white schools with the support of his teachers, aptly highlighting Washington's views as to what was possible in the North. At the age of 17, Du Bois moved to Nashville, Tennessee to study at Fisk University, and for the first time he encountered Jim Crow laws. Following graduate study in Berlin, he became the first African-American to receive a PhD from Harvard College. Nearing the turn of the century, he published *The Philadelphia Negro: A Social Study*, and coined the era's catch-phrase, "the talented tenth." This term proposed that one out of every ten black men could become a leader of his race. The premise behind such a belief was the conviction that the "Negro race, like all races, is going to be saved by its exceptional men."[58] He supported women's rights, and he founded a Pan-African Congress to help free African countries from European colonial power.

As a professor at Atlantic University, Du Bois began to attack Washington for failing to demand equality for his people. Revisiting the Atlanta speech, Du Bois openly "deplored"[59] the emphasis on vocational skills to the neglect of intellectual ascendancy and the demand for civil rights. Washington's projects were all too silent on social crises as the subject of race itself was "systematically excluded."[60] Further, Washington's comfort around influential whites from whom black institutions might receive funds, government patronage and support was to the activists the same as asking the master for freedom. In the onslaught against "accommodation," Du Bois attempted to strip away the niceties that suggested political and business acumen, good collaboration, and successful development. For Du Bois, these were different masks chosen and worn for specific audiences, putting forth the necessary rhetoric to gain the rewards while omitting even minor slights, much less horrific violations of black people's civil rights. The activists saw Washington donning the mask of the "bargainer"[61] in his dealings with white philanthropists and government officials.

This debate, which would rage for decades, was likely to be a "winner-take-all" despite the fact that the two men's original goals were "not fundamentally incompatible."[62] Washington's alleged abandonment of higher education and civil equality in the immediate appeared as nothing more than the "seeming acceptance of segregation."[63] As the debate heightened, that perception worsened. Washington's "bourgeois, anti-labor, anti-democratic appeal"[64] became the public emblem for separating the races. Du Bois emphasized the point that Washington's fundraising success came not only from the wrong master, but that it was attained by "ruthless and duplicitous means."[65] Washington's only outer show of defense was again to remind Northerners that the real world in the South was far different than theirs, and that he, not they, had a precious institution to protect. In *Up from History*, Robert J. Norrell's biography of Washington, the author upholds Washington's point on that score. Norrell asserts that even though the ideas of self-help for the Southern blacks were reduced by some social scientists into accommodation, his

[58] Frontline, *Booker T. Washington and W.E.B. Du Bois* –www.pbs.org/wgbh/pages/frontline/shows/race/etc/road.html

[59] Encyclopaedia Britannic, *Booker T. Washington, American Educator*, May 20, 2018 – www.britannica.com/biography/Booker-T-Washington

[60] Encyclopaedia Britannica

[61] Shelby Steele, NY Times

[62] Shelby Steele, , Pride and Compromise, *Sunday Book Review*, Feb. 12, 2009, New York Times –
www.nytimes.com/2009/02/15/books/reviews/steele-t-html

[63] History.com

[64] History.com

[65] History.com

perseverance was actually a "rather brave and pro-black position."[66] The charge of wearing the bargainer's mask does carry the "taint"[67]of "Uncle Tomism,"[68] but Norrell rejected the term entirely, comparing Washington's style to that of a "fox."[69] He further asserted that what Du Bois refused to consider is that when conditions are forced on one, and destruction is the clear wage of resistance, it is "coercion."[70] In employing the term, he informed Northern critics that the South during Washington's era was "not terribly far from 'final solution' thinking."[71] Washington, he contends, did what was left to him by simply asking his people to openly compete with others. He further argued that bargaining from a straight-across position if possible does not lack integrity, but Du Bois employed the darker meaning by likening Washington to a sycophant.

Du Bois was joined in the fight against Washington by fellow Harvard graduate William Monroe Trotter, the first black Phi Beta Kappa graduate and a journalist with clout of his own. In 1901, Trotter co-founded the Boston Literary and Historical Association, and with colleague George Forbes, he established *The Guardian* newspaper in order to disseminate "propaganda against discrimination."[72] In 1903, Washington was invited to speak at the AME Zion Church of Boston, and during the event, Trotter began to question him. The result was a shouting match so explosive that it was affectionately dubbed by the press as "The Boston Riot."[73] Trotter became so belligerent that he was arrested and jailed for a month. He took this free time to read Du Bois' book, *The Souls of Black Folks*.

---

[66] Shelby Steele
[67] Shelby Steele
[68] Shelby Steele
[69] Shelby Steele
[70] Shelby Steele
[71] Shelby Steele
[72] Biography, William Monroe Trotter – www.biography.com/people/william-monroe-trotter-9510831
[73] Biography, William Monroe Trotter

Trotter

Once released, he co-established the Negro Suffrage League and worked with Du Bois on the Niagara Movement, an assembly of black American leaders gathering in Canada where no government suppression could deter them. Together, they produced a manifesto personally claiming "every single right that belongs to a freeborn American, political and social."[74] Du Bois and Monroe went so far as to imply that in his iron rule of Tuskegee and other pet projects, Washington had employed a "brand of boss politics,"[75] much like a master himself. The two believed that in Washington's sphere of influence, even the more idealistic young were ostracized if they strayed from accommodation to activism. Authors given the luxury of hindsight insist that in opposition to Du Bois and Trotter, Washington did not tacitly accept Jim Crow and its attending violence, nor did he fail to respond. Behind his "deliberate ambiguity,"[76] he secretly worked against the system, in large part with financial power, the chosen language for his belief system. His background with presidents belied a pragmatic success in advising against disbanding colored troops by either federal or state edict, and his graduates went into the world to work as artisans. To supporters and admirers, Washington was the very epitome of the self-made man hailing from an environment in which accomplishing that was all but impossible for black people, whereas the Northern critics, for all their well-deserved ire toward the system, did not originate there. Some scholars would likely agree that to call for martyrdom from 2,000 miles away while a tangible, constructive alternative was available required no courage, only scheduling a speech or publishing an article.

[74] Biography, William Monroe Trotter
[75] History.com
[76] History.com

As impatience grew among other black leaders, Washington's relevance to the budding civil rights movement dwindled, and more militant individuals took his place in the public consciousness. Many never forgave him for failing to speak out immediately against lynching and voting barriers, and his mission of self-advancement became lost for a time in the racial maelstrom, as the young began to perceive him as a "relic from another era"[77] and a hindrance to the movement. Du Bois and Trotter became the new faces of equal opportunity for blacks in America.

1909 saw the establishment of the National Association for the Advancement of Colored People following an outbreak of violence in Springfield, Illinois the year before. The NAACP was originally established as a biracial group, but Trotter refused to ally himself with Du Bois' inspiration unless an all-black component was installed to focus on black opportunity and freely express itself in its own community.

All the while, Du Bois continued to eliminate a vanquished Washington from the equation, declaring that his "large financial responsibilities have made him dependent on the rich charitable public."[78] Raising a profile of Washington as a bargainer with ulterior motives, Du Bois accused his nemesis as a half-truth teller, speaking in partial terms before each audience but intending to "appear as the whole truth."[79] He added in conflicting terms that Washington lamentably placed personal advancement ahead of politics, despite being "the most important black political broker of his day."[80] In tandem with the commentary on Washington's indifference to politics, Du Bois heightened the irony by concluding, "Oh, Washington was a politician."[81] The famous debates between the two men, in the light of a changing social preference, often left Washington appearing as the one selling his people down the river and preaching for a style of education that had long become irrelevant. Hammering on the despotic realities behind Washington's quiet manner, Du Bois asserted that his nemesis "made and broke men and institutions with a nod of his head."[82]

If there was truth to that assessment, the opposite trend pointed to a breakdown of Washington's authority even at Tuskegee, which experienced instances of unrest. The intricate, unbending system of rules fell hard on a new sort of student who was less directly attached to the days of slavery. A sense of defeatism could be detected in the school's atmosphere, and the administration operated under previously unknown pressure. On one of Washington's trips to New York on March 18, 1911, he was brutally assaulted and severely beaten in a West 63rd Street hallway by a man, and to just about everyone's general amazement, Washington supported the dropping of all charges. He even reportedly claimed that he likely deserved the beating,

---

[77] Patricia Daniels
[78] John Simkin
[79] John Simkin
[80] Sherman Jones
[81] Sherman Jones
[82] Sherman Jones

accepting that the assailer, a Mr. Ulrich, acted under the impression that Washington was a prowler and did what was necessary to keep his daughter safe after kidnapping threats were made against her. The result of the incident served to bring Washington and the NAACP into a somewhat closer relationship.

A picture of Washington speaking at Carnegie Hall in New York City in 1909

By the 1910s, Washington was in his mid-50s, and the anxiety of the struggles from the last half century began to take its toll on his physical condition. He developed high blood pressure and kidney disease, falling seriously on another trip to New York City in November 1915. Taken to St. Luke's Hospital, he was diagnosed with arteriosclerosis and warned to put his affairs in order. Wishing to die at home, Washington, with his wife Margaret, boarded a train headed for Tuskegee on November 14. Upon arrival, he was in an unconscious state, and he died at 4:45 in the morning.

More than 8,000 people gathered in and around Tuskegee Institute Chapel for Washington's funeral. He was interred on a gentle hill overlooking the campus in a brick tomb fashioned by his students. Washington's grave is now a National Historic Site open to the public.

A picture of Washington's funeral procession

Following his death, Washington's hold on the imaginations of Southern blacks was broken. Having endured what they could, they now sought to escape Jim Crow. In the years leading up to the 20th century, the South contained 90% of the country's black population, but great numbers sought a more welcoming life by moving north in an epic migration. Washington's theory of collaborative accommodation did not survive the sensibilities of the following generation, and while the concept economic self-reliance continued to endure, it was forever mixed with an insistence that American law apply equally to all citizens.

Tuskegee itself has not faded as Washington's premier accomplishment. In the year of his death, the campus sported 100 well-equipped buildings, a student body of 1,500, a faculty of over 200, a curriculum of 29 trades and professions available for study, and an endowment of $2 million.

W.E.B. Du Bois may have won the day when it came to the equality movement, but his influence all but ended when he went too far in embracing communism and made the mistake of hailing Soviet leader Joseph Stalin as a "great man."[83]

---

[83] Jim Powell

The release of the blockbuster film *Birth of a Nation* in 1915 would have stung Washington to the core. In D.W. Griffith's ode to the Jim Crow era, the film glamorized a nation of "heroic klansmen"[84] keeping the streets safe from "wild"[85] marauding negroes in a heroic attempt to preserve white civilization.

Ultimately, the debate between whether a subverted society should work its way into respectability or rebel, choosing between "catching up" or wresting equality from the hands of white masters, fell silent. Others took up the banner of each camp, and some of the most notable mixed the two ideologies. Authors such as Charles Johnson vindicated Washington without having to prove him right in the conflict with Du Bois, and even today, Washington is hailed by the *Journal of Education* as the man who launched "the Negro Renaissance in the South."[86] Peers continued to laud him as a man of "incorrigible humility" and "indisputably a man of the folk."[87] His lesser known work on behalf of Africa came to recognition, as few realized he had fought to defend the integrity of the Liberian nation.

Whatever the activists' charges against his integrity, Washington's demeanor unfailingly reflected the core of his convictions. For any public occasion, his mode of dress was always that of "a prosperous peasant,"[88] and no matter the location or the honor, "his heart was always at Tuskegee."[89] In her recollection of time spent serving Washington's mission as a teacher, Natalie Lord recalled, "I can see his figure, his strong, expressive face, and hear his voice, so powerful and earnest when a thought required it, yet gentle and tender…"[90]

Booker T. Washington became the first black man to be featured on a United States postal stamp in 1940, and in 1946, his likeness was imprinted on the memorial half-dollar. His boyhood home at Hale's Ford is now a National Park, built for the centennial of his birth, and the monument erected to his honor at Tuskegee is centered on a phrase, "Lifting the Veil," and reads, "A race, like an individual, lifts itself up by lifting others up."[91] Washington is pictured lifting the heavy fabric of ignorance from the eyes of his people.

By the 1970s, following the death of Martin Luther King, Jr., some writers claimed Washington's "standing among scholars is fairly low,"[92] despite King's insistence on kindness and generous, respectful participation between the races. Some authors such as Adolph Reed Jr.

---

[84] Lawrence J. Friedman, Life "In the Lion's Mouth": Another Look at Booker T. Washington. *The Journal of Negro History*, Vol. 59 No. 4 (October, 1974) pp337-351, University of Chicago Press Journals

[85] Lawrence J. Friedman

[86] Journal of Education, 1896

[87] Journal of Education, 1896

[88] Jim Powell

[89] Pero Gaglo Dagbovie, Exploring a Century of Historical Scholarship on Booker T. Washington, University of Chicago Press Journals, *The Journal of African American History*, Vol. 92 No. 2 (Spring, 2007) pp239-264

[90] Jim Powell

[91] Black Past.org

[92] Pero Gaglo Dagbovie

still cast him as a "freelance race spokesman"[93] dependent on white concurrence and a "celebration of those folks who go along to get along."[94] Supreme Court Justice Clarence Thomas, who according to Reed operated in the same way with great success, is a modern-day example. Washington is harshly portrayed as an endearingly challenged "turn-of-the-century Forrest Gump,"[95] but no evidence of such challenges were ever uncovered in his lifetime.

Author Monroe N. Work took Washington far more seriously as a "pioneer."[96] Monroe's message is straightforward in asserting that Washington, rather than abide by a standard curriculum, made a study of the condition of his people and created a curriculum to fit their needs. He was, in Monroe's view, original and intuitive, and the way he navigated the diverse public opinion was an inescapable reality. Black people first introduced to his ideas often asked why he wanted to teach their children to work, as they had always worked. They wanted to be free and "live like white folks without working."[97] Some whites were violently opposed to any form of black education, while others asked if he intended to train preachers, teachers and servants. Such a regimen was virtuous to the Southern whites, and even in the North, many assumed that an educated black was still intended to serve as "a mere hewer of wood and drawer of water."[98] Washington did not answer these mindsets to gain popularity, but to alter deep-seated myths. He taught that work did not equal slavery, even as the Bible supported punitive labor for a disobedient Adam and Eve. Washington lectured that nobility lay in "the sweat of the brow."[99] He preached constantly, even to those with no interest in education, that life-related learning should be "as common as the grass."[100] In addition to Tuskegee's many extension programs, all products of Washington's mind before the start of the First World War, the school added a hospital and nurse training school in later years, drastically reducing the death rate in the area.

More recent writers believe Washington's early environment under the employ of the Ruffner family was not a barrier to advancement but something that offered him an opportunity. His goals were, according to written accounts, increasingly encouraged by the family, and such early impressions likely reinforced Washington's less belligerent relationship with whites because he was treated kindly by all accounts. In retrospect, Washington spoke of his association with Louis and Viola Knapp Ruffner as a friendship, and by most accounts, the Ruffner family served as a boon to Washington's zeal for obtaining an education. Washington certainly behaved as a grateful recipient, corresponding with the family until his death.

---

[93] Pero Gaglo Dagbovie
[94] Pero Gaglo Dagbovie
[95] Pero Gaglo Dagbovie
[96] Monroe N. Work, Booker T. Washington, Pioneer, *The Journal of Social Forces* Vol. 3 No. 2 (January, 1925), Oxford University Press.
[97] Monroe N. Work
[98] Monroe N. Work
[99] Monroe N. Work
[100] Monroe N. Work

In 1999, the relationship was revived between descendants of both families. Two of Washington's granddaughters were located, and they received invitations to a Ruffner family reunion held in Lancaster, Ohio. Edith Washington Johnson and Margaret Washington Clifford responded favorably, and the families met. Between June 21 and 23, a second reunion was held in Charleston, West Virginia. The families had come together 140 years prior. At the 2002 annual meeting of the Kanawha Salines Presbyterian Church of Malden, a joint memorial service was held for Edith Washington Johnson, who died on January 6 of that year, and Doris Laver Ruffner, who died on April 6. Doris was the co-author of the family biography, *Peter Ruffner and his Descendants*, with Olivia Taylor Ruffner. Following the service, both families were invited to the home of West Virginia Senator Larry Rowe, then to the Embassy Suites for a reception in honor of the Booker T. Washington reunion. At that gathering, special remarks were offered by Charles Hughes, Edith's son, along with an address by Margaret Washington Clifford and Eric Hughes. A discussion of Olivia Davidson Washington's influence at Tuskegee was held, and the Ruffner family then made a donation to Tuskegee University. A few members of the Ruffner family went on to the West Virginia State Capital not far from Ruffner State Park. The Washington family later gathered for a photo near the spot, also known as Rifleman's Park. They were invited to the Joseph Ruffner Log Cabin for refreshments before moving on to visit the Washington ancestral home.

In the modern age, the overly simple analyses directed against Washington are undergoing reinterpretation for generations that were born a century after. He remains one of the only African-Americans commonly profiled as a great leader in school textbooks, and as a figure at the forefront of social ideology after the Civil War, his life remains a crucial study, even as his legacy remains the topic of heated debate. Booker T. Washington has been philosophically "abused,"[101] according to Work and later biographers, and many now believe that he did not subscribe to "surrender,"[102] a charge leveled in the midst of a populist wave triggered by anti-black violence. Lawrence Friedman, author of *Life in the Lion's Mouth*, may have put Booker T. Washington's various relationships with whites and blacks of all backgrounds in an enhanced but delicate perspective, considering the racial baggage of the famous old stories originating in Africa. He was not anyone's black Christ, nor was he an Uncle Tom, "but a cunning Brer Rabbit, born and bred in the briar patch of tangled American race relations."[103]

Online Resources

Other books about 19th century America by Charles River Editors

Other books about 20th century America by Charles River Editors

---

[101] Monroe N. Work

[102] Monroe N. Work

[103] Lawrence J. Friedman

Other books about Booker T. Washington on Amazon

Further Reading

American Historama, Compromise of 1877 – www.american-historama.org/1866-1881/Compromise-of-1877.htm

AAREG, Olivia Davidson Washington, Quiet Co-Founder of Tuskegee, November 11, 1854 – www.aaregistry.org/story-olivia-davidson-washington-quiet-cofounder-of-tuskegee/

Biography, George Washington Carver- www.biography.com/people/george-washington-carver-9240299

BlackPast.org., Hampton University (1868 - -) – www.blackpast.org/aah/hampton-university

BlackPast.org., Washington, Booker T., (1856-1915) – www.blackpast.org/aah/washington-booker-t-1856-1915

Brooks, Erik F., Booker T. Washington, The Encyclopedia of Alabama, Georgia Southern University – www.encyclopediaofalabama.org/article/h-1506

BTW Society, Booker T. Washington Society, Honorary Master's Degree Conferred by Harvard College, June 24, 1896 – www.btwsociety.org/library/honors/01.php

Calista, Donald, Booker T. Washington, Another Look, the University of Chicago Press Journals, *The Journal of Negro History*, Vol. 149, No. 4 (October, 1964)

Croom, Barry D., Agricultural Education at the Tuskegee Normal and Industrial School, North Caroline State University – www.files.eric.edu.gov/fulltext/EJ840076.pdf

Daniels, Patricia, Booker T. Washington, Black Educator and Founder of Tuskegee Institute, thoughtco.com, April 7, 2017 update –www.thoughtco.com/booker-t-washington-1799859

Dagbovie Pero Gaglo, Booker T. Washington, Exploring a Century of Historical Scholarship, *The Journal of African American History* Vol. 91 No. 2 (Spring, 2007)

Encyclopaedia Britannica, John D. Rockefeller –www.britannica.com/biography/John-D-Rockefeller

Encyclopaedia Britannica, Booker T. Washington, American Educator, May 10, 2018 – www.britannica.com/biography/Booker-T-Washington

Foner, Eric, Garraty, John A., Eds., Booker T. Washington, history.com/topics/black-history/booker-t-washington

Friedman, Lawrence J., Life "In the Lion's Mouth": Another Look at Booker T. Washington, *The Journal of Negro History*, Vol. 59, No. 4 (October, 1974), University of Chicago Press Journals

Frontline, Booker T. Washington and W.E.B. Du Bois – www.pbs.org/wgbh/pages/frontline/shows/race/etc/road.html

Gibson, Robert A., Booker T. Washington and W.E.B. Du Bois: The Problem of Negro leadership, Yale. New Haven Teachers Institute – www.teachersinstitute.edu/curriculum/units/1978/2/78.02.02xhtml

History, Plessy v Ferguson – www.history.com/topics/blak-history/plessy-v-ferguson

Jones, Sherman, Review of Booker T. Washington: A Powerful and Multi-Faceted Politician by Louis Harlan and Raymond W. Smock, *Change*, Vol. 14, No. 3 (April, 1982)

Journal of Education, Booker T. Washington, Volume XLIV, No. 13, 1896, Trustees of Boston University

Lewis, Femi, National Negro Business League: Fighting Jim Crow with Economic Development – www.thoughtco.com/nationa-negro-business-league-45289

Lewis, Jone Johnson, Margaret Murray Washington, First Lady of Tuskegee, Thoughto.com-www.thoughtco.com/margaret-murray-washington-3528124

McNamara, Robert, Compromise of 1877: Set Stage for Jim Crow Era – www.thought.co.com/the-Compromise-of-1877-after-the-civil-war-1773369

National Park Service, Booker T. Washington – www.nps.gov/bowa/a-birthplace-that-experienced-slavery-the-war-and-emancipation.htm

Newikis, Fannie Smith Washington – www.newikis.com/en/wiki/Fannie_Smith_Washington

NNDB, Anna T. Jeanes – www.nndb.com/people/076/000204461

Powell, Jim, Up from Slavery: A Biography of Booker T. Washington – www.libertarianism.org/publications/essays/slavery-biography-booker-t-washington

Ruffner Family Association, 2002, Booker T. Washington Family Reunion of Charleston, West Virginia –www.ruffnerfamily.org/wp/2002-booker-t-washington-family-reunion-charleston-wv/

Sears Archives, Julius Rosenwald (1862-1952) – www.searsarchives.com/people/juliusrosenwald.htn

Simkin, John, Booker T. Washington, Spartacus Educational – www.spartacus-education.com/USAbooks.htm

Spark notes, Up from Slavery, Booker T. Washington – www.sparknotes.com/lit/up-from-slavery/character/booker-t-washington/

Steele, Shelby, Pride and Compromise, *Sunday Book Review*, Feb 12, 2009, New York Times – www.nytimes.com/2009/02/15/books/review/Steele-t-html

University of North Carolina, Documenting the American South – www.docsouth.unc.edu/fpn/washington/bio.html

U.S. History42d.Booker T. Washington – www.ushistory.orgus/42d.asp

Work, Monroe N., Booker T. Washington, Pioneer, *The Journal of Social Forces*, Vol. 3 No. 2 (January, 1925), Oxford University Press

Wormser Richard, Booker T. Washington, The Rise and Fall of Jim Crow, Thirteen: Media with Impact – www.thirteen.org/wnet/jimcrow/stories_people_booker.html

Free Books by Charles River Editors

We have brand new titles available for free most days of the week. To see which of our titles are currently free, click on this link.

Discounted Books by Charles River Editors

We have titles at a discount price of just 99 cents everyday. To see which of our titles are currently 99 cents, click on this link.

29642916R00028

Made in the USA
Lexington, KY
01 February 2019